In The Beginning...

Scripture Memory and Writing Lessons in Standard Print Form

Genesis 1:1-31 and 2:1-3

KJV

This Book Belongs to

_____

Dear Scholar,

I have put together this Workbook to encourage the writing down and memorization of scriptures. You are encouraged to read aloud and say each verse until you are able to recite it to your teacher/parent. Writing it down will help you master the skills of writing as well as penmanship. Once you have finished this book you may wish to buy one of the other workbooks I have published, or you can of course, open your own bible and copy it into a notebook which will have the same beneficial effect.

Copywork, which is the copying down of any well written text has been shown to be beneficial in the building of healthy cognitive reflexes in the brain and is thought to boost overall literary intelligence.

Memorization of Poetry, Bible Verses or other well

written work, improves the memory and encourages overall enhancement of literacy and intelligence. As you practice remembering your verses and writing them down with care and diligence your skills in writing will improve. Practice makes perfect in writing as well as every skill you can learn.

I hope this book as well as the many other workbooks I have put together encourage life long habits in learning such as the Copying down and Memorization of Scriptures, which should be as frequent of habit as possible.

And of course I would like to dedicate this book as well as all of my other works to the glory of God. It is my utmost desire that these books bring you closer to Jesus. "Draw nigh unto God, and He will draw nigh to you." - James 4:8

-Rebecca McCaulou

Lesson 1

Memory Verse of the day

Genesis 1:1

"In the beginning God created the heaven and the earth."

Genesis 1:1

In the beginning God
created the heaven
and the earth.

Lesson 2

Memory Verse of the day

Genesis 1:2

"And the earth was without form, and void; and darkness was upon the face of the deep. And the Spirit of God moved upon the face of the waters."

Genesis 1:2 (part 1)

And the earth was without

form, and void, and

darkness was upon the

Genesis 1:2 (part 2)

face of the deep. And the

Spirit of God. moved upon

the face of the waters.

Lesson 3

Memory Verse of the day

Genesis 1:3 "And God said, Let there be light: and there was light."

Genesis 1:3

And God said, Let there be

light: and there was light.

Lesson 4

Memory Verse of the day

Genesis 1:4 "And God saw the light, that it was good: and God divided the light from the darkness."

Genesis 1:4

And God saw the light, that

it was good: and God divided

the light from the darkness.

Lesson 5

Memory Verse of the day

Genesis 1:5 "And God called the light Day, and the darkness he called Night. And the evening and the morning were the first day."

Genesis 1:5 (part 1)

And God called the light Day,
and the darkness he called
Night.

Genesis 1:5 (part 2)

And the evening and the
morning were the first
day.

Lesson 6

Memory Verse of the day

Genesis 1:6 "And God said, Let there be a firmament in the midst of the waters, and let it divide the waters from the waters."

Genesis 1:6 (part 1)

And God said, Let there be

a firmament in the midst

of the waters,

Genesis 1:6 (Part 2)

and let it divide the

waters from the waters.

Lesson 7

Name:

Memory Verse of the day

Genesis 1:7 "And God made the firmament, and divided the waters which were under the firmament from the waters which were above the firmament: and it was so."

Genesis 1:7 (part 1)

And God made the firmament,

and divided the waters which

were under the

firmament from the waters
which were above the
firmament: and it was so.

Lesson 8

Memory Verse of the day

Genesis 1:8 "And God called the firmament Heaven. And the evening and the morning were the second day."

Genesis 1:8

And God called the firmament

Heaven. And the evening and

the morning were the second

day.

Lesson 9

Memory Verse of the day

Genesis 1:9 "And God said, Let the waters under the heaven be gathered together unto one place, and let the dry land appear: and it was so."

And God said, Let the
waters under the heaven
be gathered together.

Genesis 1:9 (part 2)

unto one place, and let

the dry land appear:

and it was so.

Lesson 10

Memory Verse of the day

Genesis 1:10 "And God called the dry land Earth; and the gathering together of the waters called he Seas: and God saw that it was good."

Genesis 1:10 (part 1)

And God called the dry land

Earth; and the gathering

together of the waters

called he Seas: and God saw

that it was good.

Lesson 11

Memory Verse of the day

Genesis 1:11 "And God said, Let the earth bring forth grass, the herb yielding seed, and the fruit tree yielding fruit after his kind, whose seed is in itself, upon the earth: and it was so."

Genesis 1:11 (part 1)

And God said, Let the earth

bring forth grass, the herb

yielding seed, and the fruit

Genesis 1:11 (part 2)

tree yielding fruit after his

kind, whose seed is in itself,

upon the earth: and it was

so.

Lesson 12

Memory Verse of the day

Genesis 1:12 "And the earth brought forth grass, and herb yielding seed after his kind, and the tree yielding fruit, whose seed was in itself, after his kind: and God saw that it was good."

Genesis 1:12 (part 1)

And the earth brought forth

grass, and herb yielding seed

after his kind, and the tree

Genesis 1:12 (part 2)

yielding fruit, whose seed was

in itself, after his kind: and

God saw that it was good.

Lesson 13

Memory Verse of the day

Genesis 1:13 "And the evening and the morning were the third day."

Genesis 1:13

And the evening and the
morning were the third day.

Lesson 14

Date:

_____

Name:

_____

Memory Verse of the day

Genesis 1:14 "And God said, Let there be lights in the firmament of the heaven to divide the day from the night; and let them be for signs, and for seasons, and for days, and years:."

Genesis 1:14 (part 1)

And God said, Let there be

lights in the firmament of

the heaven to divide the day

from the night;

Genesis 1:14 (part 2)

and let them be for

signs, and for seasons,

and for days, and years:

Lesson 15

Memory Verse of the day

Genesis 1:15 "And let them be for lights in the firmament of the heaven to give light upon the earth: and it was so."

Genesis 1:15 (part 1)

And let them be for

lights in the firmament

of the heaven.

Genesis 1:15 (part 2)

to give light upon the

earth: and it was so.

Lesson 16

Date: _____

Name: _____

Memory Verse of the day

Genesis 1:16 "And God made two great lights; the greater light to rule the day, and the lesser light to rule the night: he made the stars also."

Genesis 1:16 (part 1)

And God made two great
lights; the greater light to
rule the day,

Genesis 1:16 (part 2)

and the lesser light to rule

the night: he made the.

stars also.

Lesson 17

Memory Verse of the day

Genesis 1:17 "And God set them in the firmament of the heaven to give light upon the earth,"

Genesis 1:17

And God set them in the

firmament of the heaven

to give light upon the earth,

Lesson 18

Memory Verse of the day

Genesis 1:18 "And to rule over the day and over the night, and to divide the light from the darkness: and God saw that it was good."

Genesis 1:18 (part 1)

And to rule over the

day and over the

night, and to divide

Genesis 1:18 (part 2)

the light from the

darkness: and God saw

that it was good.

Lesson 19

Memory Verse of the day

Genesis 1:19 "And the evening and the morning were the fourth day."

Genesis 1:19

And the evening and the

morning were the fourth

day.

Lesson 20

Memory Verse of the day

Genesis 1:20 "And God said, Let the waters bring forth abundantly the moving creature that hath life, and fowl that may fly above the earth in the open firmament of heaven."

And God said, Let the waters

bring forth abundantly the

moving creature that hath

Genesis 1:20 (part 2)

life, and fowl that may fly

above the earth in the open

firmament of heaven.

Lesson 21

Memory Verse of the day

Genesis 1:21 "And God created great whales, and every living creature that moveth, which the waters brought forth abundantly, after their kind, and every winged fowl after his kind: and God saw that it was good."

Genesis 1:21 (part 1)

And God created great

whales, and every living

creature that moveth,

Genesis 1:21 (part 2)

which the waters brought

forth abundantly, after

their kind,

and every winged fowl.

after his kind: and God

saw that it was good.

Lesson 22

Memory Verse of the day

Genesis 1:22 "And God blessed them, saying, Be fruitful, and multiply, and fill the waters in the seas, and let fowl multiply in the earth."

And God blessed them,

saying, Be fruitful, and

multiply,

Genesis 1:22 (part 2)

and fill the waters in the
seas, and let fowl multiply
in the earth.

Lesson 23

Memory Verse of the day

Genesis 1:23 "And the evening and the morning were the fifth day."

Genesis 1:23

And the evening and the

morning were the fifth

day.

Lesson 24

Memory Verse of the day

Genesis 1:24 "And God said, Let the earth bring forth the living creature after his kind, cattle, and creeping thing, and beast of the earth after his kind: and it was so."

Genesis 1:24 (part 1)

And God said, Let the
earth bring forth the
living creature after his
kind,

Genesis 1:24 (part 2)

cattle, and creeping thing,

and beast of the earth

after his kind: and it was

so.

Lesson 25

Memory Verse of the day

Genesis 1:25 "And God made the beast of the earth after his kind, and cattle after their kind, and every thing that creepeth upon the earth after his kind: and God saw that it was good."

Genesis 1:25 (part 1)

And God made the beast of

the earth after his kind,

and cattle after their

kind,

Genesis 1:25 (part 2)

and every thing that

creepeth upon the earth

after his kind: and God

saw that it was good.

Lesson 26

Memory Verse of the day

Genesis 1:26 "And God said, Let us make man in our image, after our likeness: and let them have dominion over the fish of the sea, and over the fowl of the air, and over the cattle, and over all the earth, and over every creeping thing that creepeth upon the earth."

Genesis 1:25 (part 1)

And God said, Let us make
man in our image, after
our likeness.

Genesis 1:25 (part 2)

and let them have dominion

over the fish of the sea,

and over the fowl of the air,

Genesis 1:25 (part 3)

and over the cattle, and

over all the earth, and

over every creeping thing

that creepeth upon the

earth."

Lesson 27

Memory Verse of the day

Genesis 1:27 "So God created man in his own image, in the image of God created he him; male and female created he them."

Genesis 1:27 (part 1)

So God created man in his
own image, in the image
of God created he him;

Genesis 1:27 (part 2)

male and female.

created he them.

Lesson 28

Date:

Name:

Memory Verse of the day

Genesis 1:28 "And God blessed them, and God said unto them, Be fruitful, and multiply, and replenish the earth, and subdue it: and have dominion over the fish of the sea, and over the fowl of the air, and over every living thing that moveth upon the earth."

Genesis 1:28 (part 1)

And God blessed them, and

God said unto them, Be

fruitful, and multiply, and

replenish the earth,

and subdue it. and have.

dominion over the fish of the

sea, and over the fowl.

Genesis 1:28 (part 3)

of the air, and over every

living thing that moveth.

upon the earth.

Lesson 29

Memory Verse of the day

Genesis 1:29 "And God said, Behold, I have given you every herb bearing seed, which is upon the face of all the earth, and every tree, in the which is the fruit of a tree yielding seed; to you it shall be for meat."

Genesis 1:29 (part 1)

And God said, Behold, I have
given you every herb.
bearing seed,

which is upon the face

of all the earth, and

every tree,

Genesis 1:29 (part 3)

in the which is the fruit of

a tree yielding seed; to you

it shall be for meat.

Lesson 30

Memory Verse of the day

Genesis 1:30 "And to every beast of the earth, and to every fowl of the air, and to every thing that creepeth upon the earth, wherein there is life, I have given every green herb for meat: and it was so."

Genesis 1:30 (part 1)

And to every beast of the earth, and to every fowl of the air,

Genesis 1:30 (part 2)

and to every thing that

creepeth upon the earth,

wherein there is life,

Genesis 1:30 (part 3)

I have given every green
herb for meat: and it was
so.

Lesson 31

Memory Verse of the day

Genesis 1:31 "And God saw every thing that he had made, and, behold, it was very good. And the evening and the morning were the sixth day."

Genesis 1:31 (part 1)

And God saw every thing

that he had made, and,

behold,

it was very good. And the

evening and the morning

were the sixth day.

Lesson 32

Memory Verse of the day

Genesis 2:1 "Thus the heavens and the earth were finished, and all the host of them. "

Genesis 2:1

Thus the heavens and
the earth were finished,
and all the host of them.

Lesson 33

Memory Verse of the day

Genesis 2:2 "And on the seventh day God ended his work which he had made; and he rested on the seventh day from all his work which he had made. "

Genesis 2:2 (part 1)

And on the seventh day

God ended his work,

which he had made;

Genesis 2:2 (part 2)

and he rested on the

seventh day from all his

work which he had made.

Lesson 34

Date:

Name:

Memory Verse of the day

Genesis 2:2 "And God blessed the seventh day, and sanctified it: because that in it he had rested from all his work which God created and made."

Genesis 2:3 (part 1)

And God blessed the

seventh day, and

sanctified it.

Genesis 2:3 (part 2)

because that in it he

had rested from all his

work which God created

and made.

Made in the USA
Las Vegas, NV
18 October 2023

79320259R00057